STUPENDOUS AND TREMENDOUS TECHNOLOGY

REMARKABLE (AND ROVING) ROBOTS

ENTER A WORLD OF MIRACULOUS MACHINES!

SONYA NEWLAND

Gareth Stevens PUBLISHING

**Please visit our website,
www.garethstevens.com.
For a free color catalog of all
our high-quality books, call
toll free 1-800-542-2595 or
fax 1-877-542-2596.**

Published in 2025 by
Gareth Stevens Publishing
2544 Clinton St.
Buffalo, NY 14224

First published in Great Britain in 2022 by Wayland

Author and editor:
Sonya Newland

Series designer:
Rocket Design (East Anglia) Ltd

Illustrator:
Steve Evans

Cataloging-in-Publication Data

Names: Newland, Sonya.
Title: Remarkable (and roving) robots / Sonya Newland.
Description: Buffalo, NY : Gareth Stevens Publishing, 2025. | Series: Stupendous and tremendous technology | Includes glossary and index.
Identifiers: ISBN 9781538294598 (pbk.) | ISBN 9781538294604 (library bound) | ISBN 9781538294611 (ebook)
Subjects: LCSH: Robots--Juvenile literature. | Robotics--Juvenile literature.
Classification: LCC TJ211.2 N48 2025 | DDC 629.8'92--dc23

Illustrations by Steve Evans: front cover main, 5t, 6b, 7, 8b, 11b, 13t, 15t, 17b, 21t, 25, 28–29 (all).

Picture acknowledgements: NASA: JSC 18b; Shutterstock: Evgenii Pavlov 4t, Phonlamai Photo 4bl, MONOPOLY919 4bm, Olga Miltsova 4br, Es sarawuth 5bl, Humberto Ramirez 5bm, Engineer studio 5br, Agor2012 6t, Blue Flourishes 8t, Art studio G 9t, Pavel Vinnik 9b, Sudowoodo 10l, bsd 10m, 10r, VectorShow 11tl, and4me 11tr, Margarita_V 12, Tartila 13bl, Visual Generation 13br, home for heroes 14t, igor malovic 14m, Fun Way Illustration 14b, lutf_fai 15b, Javvani 16, aytpark 17t, IZE-5tyle 18t, Vweiner 19, Pavlo Plakhotia 20, GUDKOV ANDREY 21b, Lecter 22t, Anton Gvozdikov 22bl, 22br, Tarikdiz 23t, BAZA Production 23b, momoforsale 24, 25, Mictoon 26t, Captain Cobi 26b, Fun Way Illustration 27t, LTDean 27b.

All additional design elements from Shutterstock or drawn by designer.

Printed in the United States of America

CPSIA compliance information: Batch #CSGS25: For further information contact Gareth Stevens at 1-800-542-2595.

REMARKABLE AND ROVING CONTENTS

ROBOT TAKEOVER!

Robots are everywhere! Look around the room – what technology can you see? Does anything move on its own? Does anything interact with you? Even the inanimate objects were probably made by robots!

WHAT IS A ROBOT?

In simple terms, robots are machines that do work. They're useful gadgets that interact with and respond to the world around them. When you think of a robot, you probably imagine it as a machine that looks a bit like a human, but in fact most robots aren't humanoid. Their size, shape, and design all depend on the job they're created to do.

WHAT CAN ROBOTS DO?

The short answer? Almost everything! Robots help humans in hundreds of different ways. They can …

BUILD THINGS

FIX THINGS (AND PEOPLE)

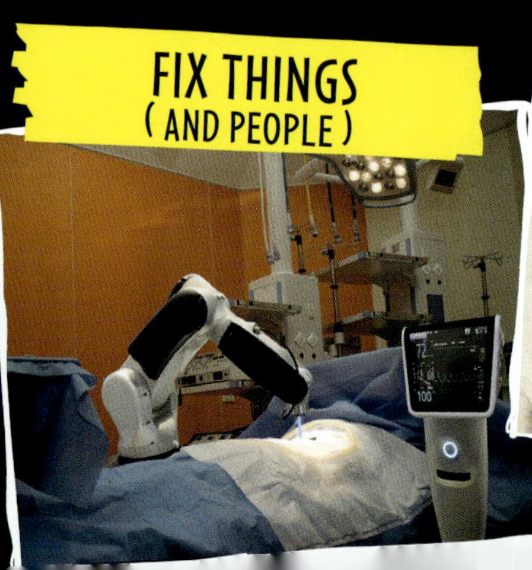

CLEAN THINGS

WHEN WERE ROBOTS INVENTED?

Robots may seem like cutting-edge tech. But in fact, toys that could move on their own were known in ancient Greece and China. We call these toys automatons, a word that comes from the ancient Greek, meaning "acting of its own will." These machines were powered by steam, water, or moving weights. Later automatons could do more complicated tasks, such as using a pen or even playing music. But robots, in the way we think of them today, need computers – so they were a long time coming!

FREAKY FACT

Leonardo da Vinci (1452–1519) was an Italian artist, engineer, scientist, and all-round genius. He designed loads of different devices, including an early android, in the form of an artificial "knight"!

WHAT IS AN AUTONOMOUS ROBOT?

Modern robots are autonomous rather than automatons! That means they can function without a lot of human input. Human engineers design and build them, of course, but after that an autonomous robot can do its job without much supervision. Some amazingly intelligent robots can even think, learn, and adapt on their own!

DELIVER THINGS

EXPLORE THINGS

SAVE THINGS

BODY AND MIND

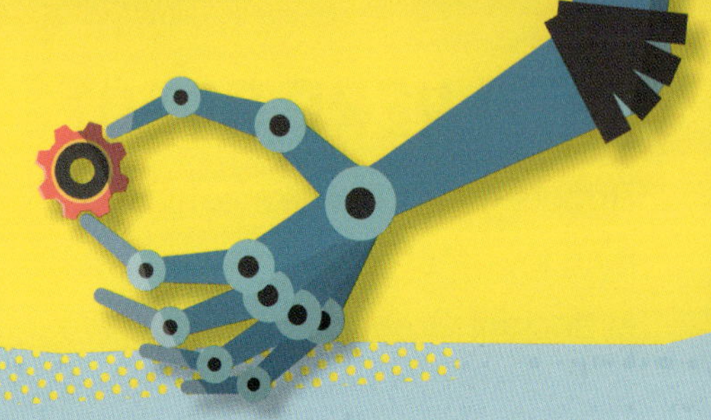

Robots usually have three types of components: controllers, mechanics, and sensors. You can think of these like the different systems that make up the human body – the brain, internal organs, limbs, senses, and so on. They all do different jobs, but they work together to allow the robot to function.

HOW DOES A ROBOT'S BRAIN WORK?

The controller is like the robot's brain – it sends messages that tell the robot what to do. The controller is actually a computer program. Like a real human brain, the computer program that controls a robot is extremely complex. It gives thousands of different commands, which the robot's moving parts follow to perform the task the robot is designed to do.

WHAT ARE MECHANICS?

A robot's mechanics are all of its moving parts – the robot equivalent of arms and legs, organs, muscles, and other human parts that twist, turn, bend, or move in any way. In a robot, these parts might be wheels, motors, pistons, gears, or grippers, or they could be more human-like features, such as a hand with fingers.

WHY DOES A ROBOT HAVE SENSORS?

Most robots have at least some simple sensors, which allow them to "read" and understand their surroundings so they don't keep bumping into things. But some robots have more advanced sensors that allow them to see, hear, and touch things in a similar way to human senses (see pages 10–11).

ROBOT ANATOMY

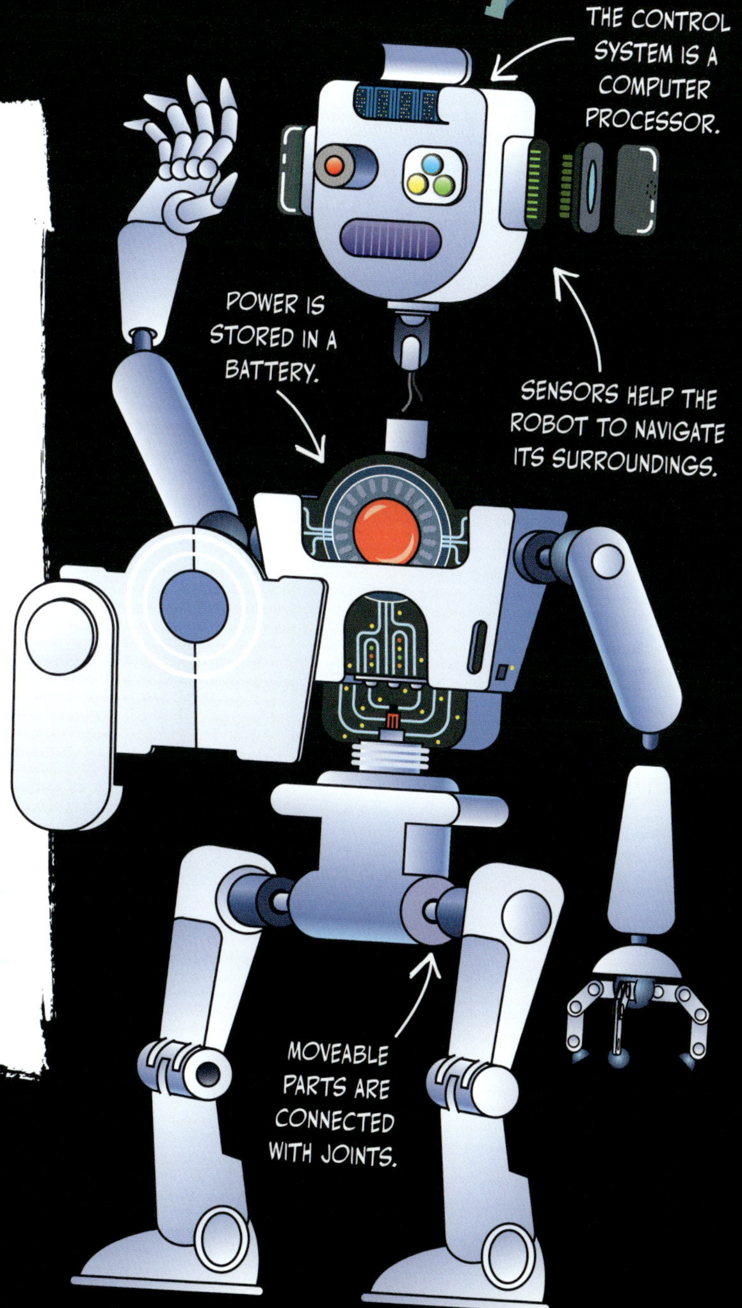

THE CONTROL SYSTEM IS A COMPUTER PROCESSOR.

POWER IS STORED IN A BATTERY.

SENSORS HELP THE ROBOT TO NAVIGATE ITS SURROUNDINGS.

MOVEABLE PARTS ARE CONNECTED WITH JOINTS.

SUPER SCIENCE

Algorithms are a computer science essential! Without these important sets of instructions, computer systems wouldn't work. In robotics, algorithms are part of a robot's controller. They can be designed to tell the machine how to behave in different situations. For example, an algorithm tells a robotic arm on a factory assembly line what piece to select, when to do so, and where to put it on the product being assembled.

INPUT AND OUTPUT

To perform tasks successfully, robots work on a system of inputs and outputs. Input is all the stuff that humans put in to the controller to tell the robot what to do. Output is the result – the task the robot does.

HOW DO ROBOTS PROCESS FEEDBACK?

An autonomous robotic system works on a "feedback loop." This means that some of the output goes back into the machine as input, which helps it to learn and adapt its actions. So, next time, the output might be slightly different.

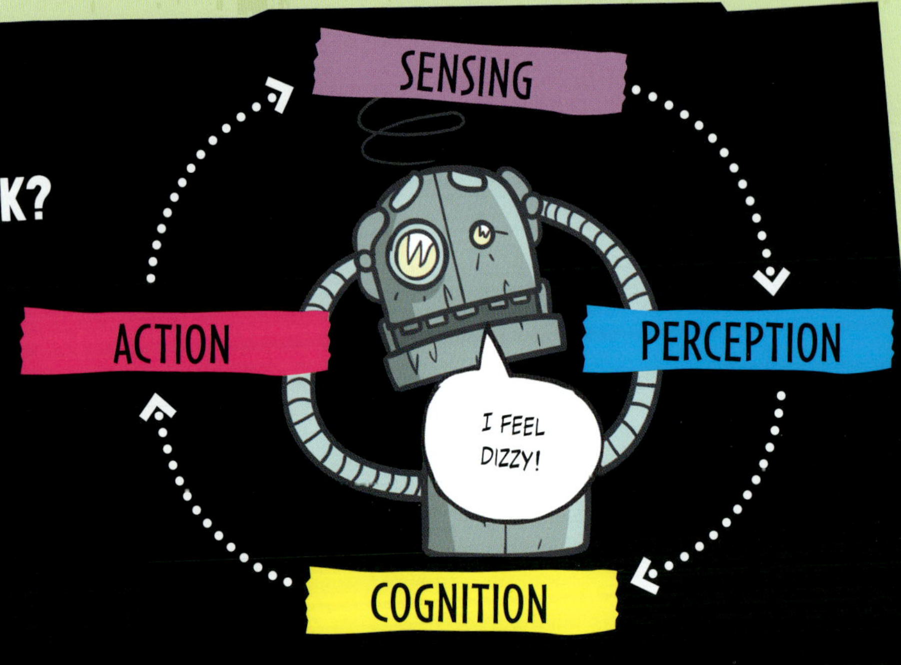

WHAT IS PERCEPTION?

In humans, perception is the way we interpret the information that our senses have gathered. Perception works in a similar way in robots. Sensors receive information from a robot's surroundings – for example, they sense if an obstacle is in the way, how hot or cold the room is, or what kind of surface the robot is moving over. Algorithms (see page 7) interpret that raw data into "real" information, so the robot perceives its environment.

WHAT IS COGNITION?

Cognition is thinking and understanding. In a robot, this means analyzing the information it has perceived or what instructions mean, and deciding what to do with the information. Once those decisions have been made, the robot performs the action – it carries out the task or reacts to the information in a particular way.

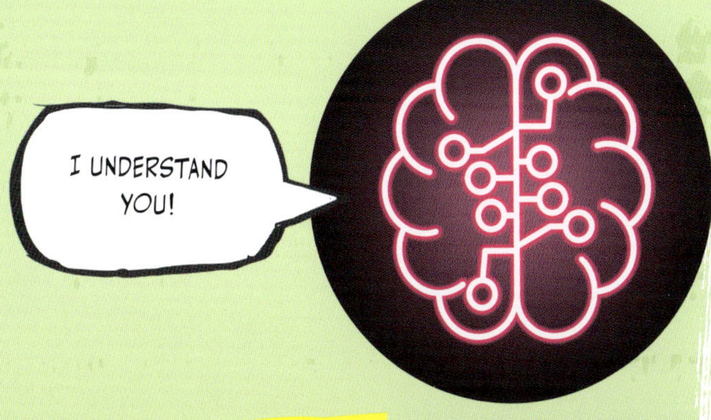

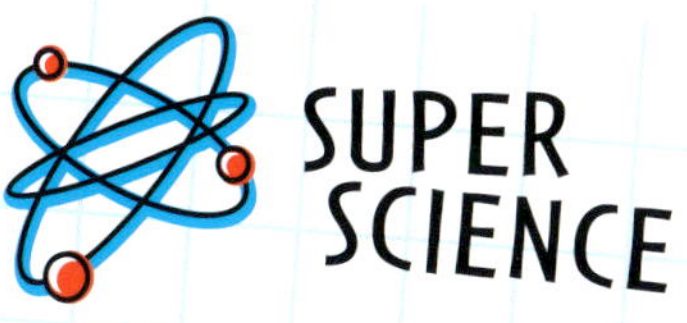

Feedback loops aren't limited to computers and other technology. In fact, they're taking place in nature all the time – biology is filled with feedback loops! For example, a cut will cause you to start bleeding. When body tissue is damaged like this, a chemical is released that activates platelets in the blood. The platelets release a chemical that instructs more platelets to be released. The loop continues until the platelets help to form a blood clot and the cut heals.

Here's how cognition works with an autonomous (self-driving) car.

1 SENSING

SENSORS, SUCH AS CAMERAS, RADAR, AND LIGHT SENSORS, GATHER INFORMATION FROM THE SURROUNDINGS.

2 PERCEPTION

ALGORITHMS CONVERT THIS INFORMATION INTO REAL THINGS, SUCH AS OTHER CARS, ROAD SIGNS, PEDESTRIANS, AND ROAD CONDITIONS.

3 COGNITION

THE CONTROL CENTER INTERPRETS THIS INFORMATION AND MAKES DECISIONS ABOUT HOW TO ACT BASED ON IT.

4 ACTION

THE MOVING PARTS OF THE CAR ACT BASED ON THOSE DECISIONS – FOR EXAMPLE, STOPPING AT A RED LIGHT.

ROBOT SENSES

Sensors are a key part of any robot – and one of the features that sets them apart from other machines. Super sensors allow robots to understand their environment. They can also mimic human senses, such as touch and sight.

HOW DO ROBOTS FEEL AND SEE?

A robot wouldn't be much use if it was constantly crashing into things (unless that's its job, of course!). That's why touch or "bump" sensors are a key part of even quite simple robots. In some ways, sensors are like sight too. They can work with cameras to allow a machine to "see" things around it.

SIMPLE ROBOTS HAVE INFRARED OR ULTRAVIOLET SENSORS. THESE SEND OUT A BEAM OF SOUND OR LIGHT AND THEN DETECT THE BEAM WHEN IT BOUNCES BACK OFF AN OBJECT.

MORE SOPHISTICATED ROBOTS MAY HAVE STEREO VISION – TWO CAMERAS THAT WORK TOGETHER TO GIVE THE MACHINE DEPTH PERCEPTION.

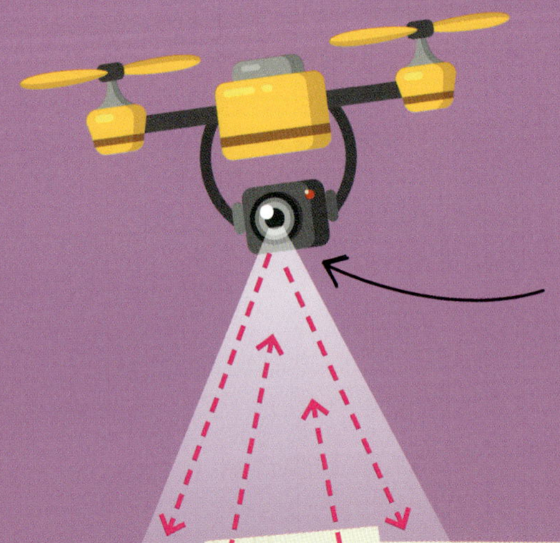

SOME ROBOTS USE A LASER SENSOR TECHNOLOGY CALLED LIDAR – LIGHT DETECTION AND RANGING. THE ROBOT SENDS OUT LASERS THAT LIGHT UP OBJECTS, AND REFLECT THE LIGHT BACK. USING THESE REFLECTIONS, THE ROBOT CAN CREATE A MAP OF ITS SURROUNDINGS SO IT KNOWS WHERE THINGS ARE.

CAN ROBOTS REALLY "HEAR"?

Do you use a virtual personal assistant? If so, you probably use a "wake word" to get its attention and then speak to it like it's a person, asking it questions or giving it commands. Every time you do that, you're interacting with a "hearing" robot. Virtual personal assistants interpret voice commands to answer questions and carry out tasks. Microphones are like a robot's ears, but computer software is what allows the gadget to understand and interpret language.

HOW CAN I HELP YOU TODAY?

WHAT OTHER SENSES CAN ROBOTS HAVE?

The human senses of smell and taste might not seem too important for robots – after all, machines don't need to eat! But robots that could taste or smell could be very useful. For example, the police use animals with a great sense of smell, such as dogs, to sniff out hidden drugs or to track down people. Robots that could smell could do the same thing. And what about a robot that could test food to see if someone might have an allergic reaction to it? That kind of technology could save lives!

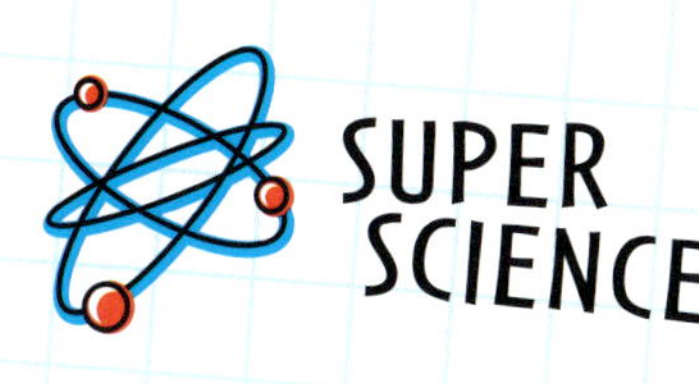

Electronic noses are a real thing! These strange sensing devices can detect and identify smells and flavors. They're already being used in many different scientific fields, but they could be life-savers when it comes to medicine. E-noses can already smell certain types of bacteria and can identify some infections by sniffing human poop!

HARD AT WORK

The original idea of robots was to make people's lives easier. That mostly meant doing the boring or dangerous jobs that humans didn't want to do! Today, robots are put to use in many different ways in many different workplaces.

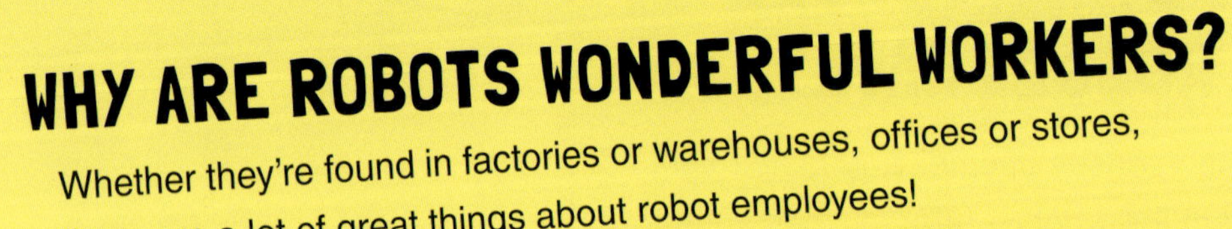

WHY ARE ROBOTS WONDERFUL WORKERS?

Whether they're found in factories or warehouses, offices or stores, there are a lot of great things about robot employees!

☒ Robots don't need to sleep or eat.

☒ They don't get bored.

☒ They never ask for a day off.

☒ They never complain about their colleagues.

☒ And they very rarely make mistakes.

BUT … It's not all good news. Just as humans hurt themselves or get ill, robots can break or go wrong.

HOW DO ROBOTS HELP IN FACTORIES?

Robots are a common sight in factories. These machines are known as industrial robots, and they're often used for repetitive tasks on production lines, such as building, spraying, welding, and labeling. They're also perfectly suited to lifting and moving heavy objects that we humans are too weak to shift around! And they're especially good at precision tasks, such as putting tiny components on circuit boards.

FREAKY FACT

Cobots – short for "collaborative robots" – are machines that are especially designed to work safely alongside humans in the workplace. Clever cobots can sense changes in their working environment, such as if a person is nearby, and change their behavior accordingly.

ROTATING

UP AND DOWN

BACKWARD AND FORWARD

REVOLVING

HOW DO ROBOTIC ARMS WORK?

In places such as factories, robots often look like giant arms. That's because robotics is all about efficiency. There's no point in giving a robot wheels or legs if it's staying in one place! However, most of these types of robots have a wide range of other movements.

RISKY BUSINESS

Robots actually do some of the most difficult and dangerous jobs you can imagine. That's because they can be specially built to go places that humans can't – and to handle materials that are too dangerous for humans to touch.

HOW DO ROBOTS HELP IN THE POLICE AND MILITARY?

Because robots can't die and because they can work very precisely, the military and the police use them for risky jobs, such as bomb disposal. Technically speaking, bomb disposal robots are actually drones – machines that are controlled by humans from a distance, rather than making decisions for themselves. Machines have been doing this dangerous job for nearly 40 years. One of the first bomb-disposal robots was called the Wheelbarrow Mark I because it was built using the electrically powered chassis of – you guessed it – a wheelbarrow!

WHAT ABOUT FLYING DRONES?

Robots can also fly! You've probably seen people using drones to take pictures from the air, but these human-controlled robots have also changed the way that the police carry out patrol and surveillance. Drones can help the police to see into hard-to-reach places and track suspects on the run much more quickly and easily than officers on foot can. Bigger drones are used by the military for surveillance and attack in war zones.

WHAT ARE THE FUKUSHIMA ROBOTS?

Robots have been really useful in handling materials such as radioactive waste, which could cause illness or even death in humans. In 2011, an earthquake and tsunami triggered a disaster at the Fukushima Daiichi Nuclear Power Plant in Japan. Radioactive fuel leaked out of the plant, so it was very dangerous for people to go near the site. But the waste had to be cleared away. So, the Japanese authorities called in the robots! Some robots were sent in first to assess the damage and gather information before their cameras were damaged by radiation. Some parts of the site were underwater, so submersible robots were sent in to detect the radioactive fuel.

FREAKY FACT

Robots can even be used as spies! Experts are developing tiny robotic spy drones, about the size of an insect. Like their bigger cousins, these super surveillance robots can take pictures and record sounds, but the advantage is that the people being spied on won't know they're there!

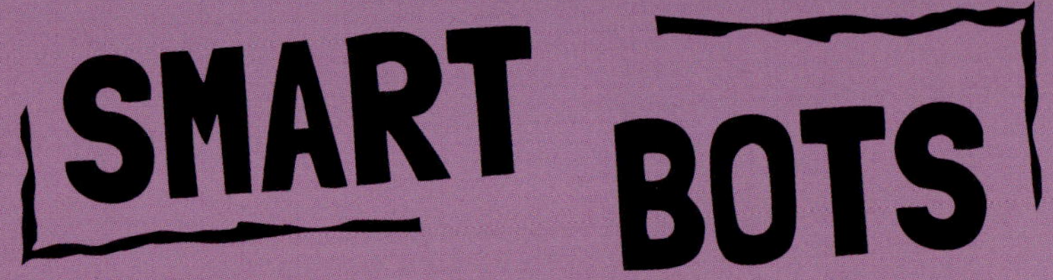

There's a difference between ordinary robots and intelligent robots. Ordinary robots are told what to do – they're programmed to behave in a certain way. Intelligent robots are, well, intelligent. They can learn and adapt on their own, just like you.

WHAT IS AI?

AI stands for "artificial intelligence." It's a term used to describe machines that use human-like intelligence to perform tasks. Amazing engineers look at human processes, such as thinking, feeling, learning, analyzing, explaining – and a whole lot more. They then try to recreate these human processes in machines so that a robot can follow similar steps to get similar results. The "intelligence" in these machines comes from extra-clever computer programs in the robot's "brain" (see page 6).

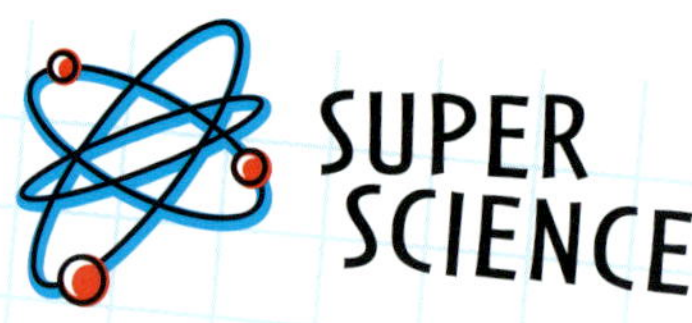

Machine learning is out there in the real world, and you use it every day. Every time you use a search engine on your computer, you're not only tapping into machine learning, you're also helping it to improve. You'll notice that over time, your computer starts predicting what you're searching for. It does that by learning from your past searches.

REMEMBER THOSE FEEDBACK LOOPS ON PAGES 8-9? THEY PLAY A BIG PART IN MACHINE LEARNING.

WHAT IS MACHINE LEARNING?

Machine learning is the science behind AI. It's what gives robots and other machines the ability to learn without being constantly reprogrammed. Think about how you learn something: a lot of the time it's trial and error. In simple terms, you learn from your mistakes. For example, if you pick up something hot, it burns your hand. Your brain remembers the pain and learns not to make that mistake again! It's a similar process in intelligent robots, although it can take longer for them to learn.

HOW DOES MACHINE LEARNING WORK?

Machine learning starts with a set of questions and answers that human programmers give the machine.

1. THE FIRST ANSWERS THE ROBOT'S BRAIN COMES UP WITH ARE JUST RANDOM GUESSES (CALLED PREDICTIONS).

2. BY RECEIVING FEEDBACK ABOUT WHICH ANSWERS WERE RIGHT AND WHICH WERE WRONG, THE COMPUTER BRAIN STARTS TO MAKE MORE EDUCATED GUESSES.

3. SLOWLY, IT MAKES FEWER AND FEWER MISTAKES BY CONSTANTLY COMPARING POSSIBLE ANSWERS WITH ONES THAT IT KNOWS ARE CORRECT.

4. THE PREDICTIONS AND OUTPUT BECOME MORE AND MORE ACCURATE.

WHY ARE ROBOTS GOOD AT GAMES?

That's not all – machine learning can go even deeper. Deep learning is a special type of machine learning that trains robots and other devices to solve problems. It does this through a neural network, which is spookily similar to the way your own brain works by sending signals via neurons (nerve cells) to different parts of your body. Thanks to deep learning, intelligent machines can make on-the-spot decisions and improve tactics based on the results of those decisions. Because computers are also excellent at making complex calculations instantly, robots can work out in a flash all sorts of possible outcomes in a game, for example. That's why computer brains are so good at strategy games like chess!

SPACE EXPLORERS

As you've seen, robots are especially useful for going to places that are tough for humans to get to or to survive in. And where could be more difficult and dangerous than outer space?

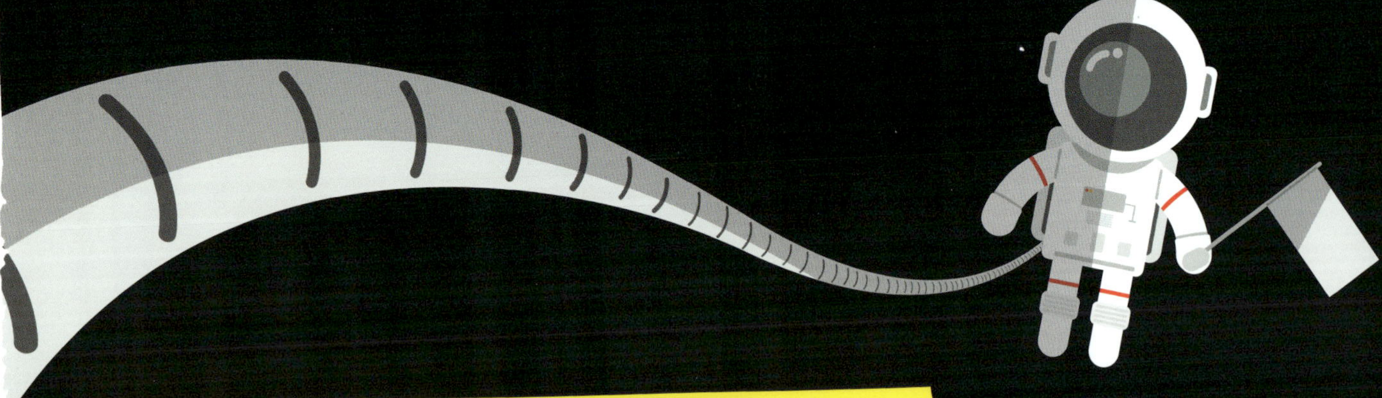

WHAT IS A ROBONAUT?

Robonauts are a type of intelligent robot created to help humans in space. While many robots don't need to look at all like us, Robonauts are deliberately designed to be physically like humans in a lot of ways. That way, they can do the same types of task that astronauts do and work alongside them. Robonauts have hands and fingers that can move in the same way as human hands, so they can grip and move objects. Cameras in their helmets allow them to "see" where they are and what they're doing.

ROBONAUTS ARE BUILT WITH A HUMANOID TOP PART THAT CAN BE ATTACHED TO WHEELS OR LEGS.

HOW MANY ROBOTS HAVE GONE TO MARS?

The Mars rovers are special robots, designed to survive the harsh conditions on the planet Mars. Unlike the Robonauts, the rovers have been to a part of space where humans have never yet set foot. The first rover, Sojourner, landed on the planet in 1997, and since then four others have made the seven-month journey to Mars: Spirit and Opportunity in 2004, Curiosity in 2012, and Perseverance in 2021. Between them, they have sent back masses of information about Mars, especially about all the types of rock that it's made of.

A HELICOPTER CALLED INGENUITY GOT A LIFT TO MARS ON THE PERSEVERANCE ROVER. IT WAS DESIGNED TO TEST THE FIRST POWERED FLIGHT ON THE RED PLANET.

LARGE, TOUGH WHEELS MEAN THE ROBOT CAN MOVE EASILY ACROSS THE ROUGH, ROCKY SURFACE OF THE PLANET.

THE ROBOTIC ARM CAN GATHER SOIL AND ROCK SAMPLES TO ANALYZE.

WHERE ELSE IN SPACE HAVE ROBOTS TRAVELED?

Space probes are autonomous spacecraft – these robotic spacecraft don't have a human pilot on board! Probes have visited every planet in the solar system, as well as moons, asteroids, and comets. They may orbit these foreign worlds and sometimes even land on them, sending information back to Earth. Two special space probes, Voyagers 1 and 2, have become the first human-made objects ever to leave our solar system. Who knows where these adventurous robots will end up?

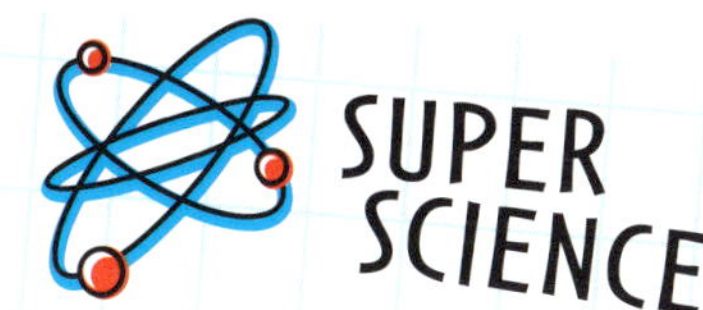

The Mars rovers aren't just about amazing technology. The information they have discovered has helped scientists in many different fields. Astronomers now know loads about this planet that was once just a dot through a telescope. Geologists can see how rocks on Earth and Mars are different – or the same. Thanks to information about Mars's atmosphere, climate scientists can make predictions about what will happen to our own planet in the future.

GOOD COMPANY

Although robots were originally invented to be the new workers of the world, they have started to become much more than that. Engineers are now designing robots with a new purpose – to take on a social role in our lives.

HOW CAN ROBOTS BE PETS?

Whether it's a cat or a dog, a guinea pig or a goldfish, we all love our pets. But looking after animals can be a big responsibility, so imagine a pet that you didn't have to remember to feed or take for a walk. Robotic pets have been designed with all the best features of our furry friends – love, loyalty, and even the ability to do tricks – but none of the drawbacks, such as cleaning up their poop or paying for a vet visit.

CAN MACHINES BE GOOD COMPANIONS?

You probably use machines to entertain yourself for hours every day, by using apps, streaming movies, or playing video games. In fact, robotic devices can play all sorts of games. Today, there are robots that are quite life-like, and some can even have conversations! As technology and AI develop, they'll have even more abilities. That will not only change the type of robots we might encounter on a day-to-day basis, but also the ways that we interact with them and how we see them.

WHY WOULD ROBOTS NEED EMOTIONS?

We humans experience a huge range of emotions. Emotional intelligence refers to the way that we're able to recognize and understand emotions, in ourselves and other people (also known as empathy). This helps us to get along with others in the real world. So, what's the point of robots having emotions? Well, think about a robot that could show human characteristics such as patience and understanding, or a robot that could read and interpret physical cues from human "friends," such as noticing if they were upset. That could really make a difference to someone who was lonely or sad.

FREAKY FACT

Animals have often been an inspiration for robotics engineers. That's partly because animal intelligence – for example, the way that apes are intelligent – is easier to recreate in machines than human intelligence but is still very effective. Other animal characteristics, such as physical strength or communities of creatures such as ants or bees working together, have helped scientists to design robots with similarly useful features.

ALMOST HUMAN

Cybernetics is the name of a complicated branch of science. It's the study of how systems use control and communication to function. By systems, we mean anything from a colony of ants to your local community! But cybernetics is also applied to machines.

WHAT ARE CYBERNETIC HUMANS?

In simple terms cybernetic humans are humanoid robots. Some of them have a human shape – two legs, two arms, and so on – but otherwise look like a more traditional robot (think C3PO from *Star Wars*). But other humanoid robots are so lifelike that you'd need to look twice to check they weren't real! These cybernetic humans have "skin" that looks and feels very realistic. Their eyes move and blink. And they may have a wide range of facial expressions, almost as if they are feeling different emotions.

CYBERNETIC HUMANS CAN LOOK REALLY REALISTIC!

THERE'S A LOT OF COMPLICATED TECH INSIDE THE HEAD OF A HUMANOID ROBOT!

I FEEL A LITTLE UNDERDRESSED!

ARE ROBOTS GOOD AT ART?

Cybernetics is all about information – getting it and using it. To be truly "human-like," robots need to learn and educate themselves. But there's a whole lot more to being human than just knowing things. We also have creativity and imagination – we can conjure ideas from our complex minds and turn them into stories, paintings, or crafts. Robots seem well adapted for practical subjects, such as math and physics, but is it possible to give them spontaneous creative ideas that will bring them one step closer to being human?

DO CYBORGS REALLY EXIST?

Cyborgs *do* exist – but not in quite the form you might imagine from sci-fi films! "Cyborg" refers to **cyb**ernetics and **org**anic material – that is, a mix of a machine and a living organism. One of the most amazing things that robotics has achieved is creating bionic limbs. These artificial arms and legs respond like real limbs do to messages from the human brain. Perhaps one day it will even be possible to implant robot brains in human bodies – or vice versa.

INCREDIBLE ROBOTIC LIMBS CAN NOW BE CONTROLLED BY MESSAGES FROM THE HUMAN BRAIN.

FREAKY FACT

A robot called Sophia (pictured left) became a citizen of Saudi Arabia in 2017 – the first ever official robot person. She works in marketing, using her own Twitter account to promote different products!

ROBOT PROBLEMS

It's easy for robots to function in environments such as factories – as we know, they're very good at repetitive tasks. The real challenge in creating more useful robots is to get them to respond naturally to things that happen when they're in an unfamiliar place.

HOW ARE HUMANS HOLDING ROBOTS BACK?

Even intelligent robots are limited by the information we give them and the jobs we tell them to do. Sometimes that's deliberate – we want them to focus on a particular task. But there are some things that even our brilliant brains don't understand, so there's no way we can program a robot's computer "brain" so that they'll get it.

There are also things that we know how to do but can't put into words. (Try explaining out loud how to ride a bike – it's very tricky!) We can't teach machines how to do things if we can't explain them clearly. But if we could create robots with truly human-like intelligence, they'd be able to learn these things for themselves, just like we do.

CAN ROBOTS MULTITASK?

A robotic vacuum cleaner is brilliant at cleaning the carpet, but probably not so good at making the bed. Although engineers are inventing amazing AI robots all the time, the fact is that – right now – most robots are designed to do a single task. They do that job really well, but they can't multitask. For robots to be completely useful in lots of different workplaces and other environments, AI technology needs to be more advanced. It may be a while yet before it has developed to a point where robots can do lots of different types of task.

CAN CARS REALLY DRIVE THEMSELVES?

Most cars already have a form of AI built in – GPS uses machine learning (see pages 16–17), which helps it to plan routes, give directions, and avoid congestion. Engineers are attempting to create fully robotic cars. Assisting human drivers with GPS technology is one thing, but a truly self-driving car has proven trickier to design! This is mainly because of the difficulties of making robots function in unfamiliar environments. Think of all the changing things a driver has to be aware of on the road: traffic lights, pedestrian crossings, intersections, traffic circles, and pedestrians and other drivers behaving unpredictably. Although the technology exists for self-driving cars, we have to ask: how safe are they really?

Robotics brings together lots of different areas of study because designing and building a robot takes lots of different skills:

 mechanical engineering to know how to design and put together the moving parts

 electrical engineering to get all the control systems working together

 computer science to build the robot's "brain" – the program that tells it what to do and how to learn

 math (especially algebra) to write the algorithms that the robot follows and to understand predictions and probabilities

 physics to figure out all the ways a robot can move and the effects that different materials and environments will have on it

THE BIG QUESTIONS

The rise of robotics has made people ask a lot of ethical questions. There's a lot we can do with the amazing technology available today, but we have to ask ourselves, is it right to do something just because we *can*?

HOW CAN WE MAKE ROBOTS THAT ARE FAIR?

Robots are created by humans, and humans have flaws. We can feel angry, frustrated, or jealous. We dislike certain things – sometimes strongly. Engineers must try to create robots that don't have negative characteristics that could cause people physical or emotional harm.

SHOULD ROBOTS BE GIVEN JOBS THAT HUMANS CAN DO?

As the science of robotics advances, more and more jobs can be done by machines. Some of them are ordinary robots and others are intelligent – but either way they're doing jobs that people once did. Should this be allowed? Or is a person's right to have a job and earn money more important than a business owner's right to make profits by using more efficient robots?

SHOULD ROBOTS HAVE RIGHTS?

If robots have feelings and emotions, should they be treated with kindness and compassion – the way we expect to be treated? Should we see them as equals? In 2017, the European Parliament decided that the amazing science of robotics had come so far that we needed to start thinking about creating laws that say what rights robots have. And if robots are intelligent enough, should they be allowed to decide their *own* rights, like we do?

RIGHTS FOR ROBOTS!

FREAKY FACT

Sci-fi writer Isaac Asimov (1920–92) created the Three Laws of Robotics in his book, *I, Robot* (1950). These fictional laws have taken on a real meaning in the modern world. They influence how scientists approach robotics in real life today. The first law is: *A robot may not injure a human being or, through inaction, allow a human being to come to harm.*

WILL ROBOTS TAKE OVER THE WORLD?

This might be the biggest question of all. What happens if robots end up being smarter than us? If robots can think, feel, reason, and adapt, what's stopping them from taking over the planet? Will humans one day be used by machines to do the jobs that they don't want to do?

Robots are already better than us at certain things, so if AI advances this *might* happen. But a lot of scientists point out that if we're clever enough to create such smart robots, we're clever enough to build in technology that makes sure they don't turn against us.

ASTONISHING ACTIVITY:
BUILD A BOT BUG

Big bots require clever computer coding, advanced electronics, and all sorts of sensors and moving parts. But you can practice being a robotics engineer by starting small and building a little bot bug to master the basics.

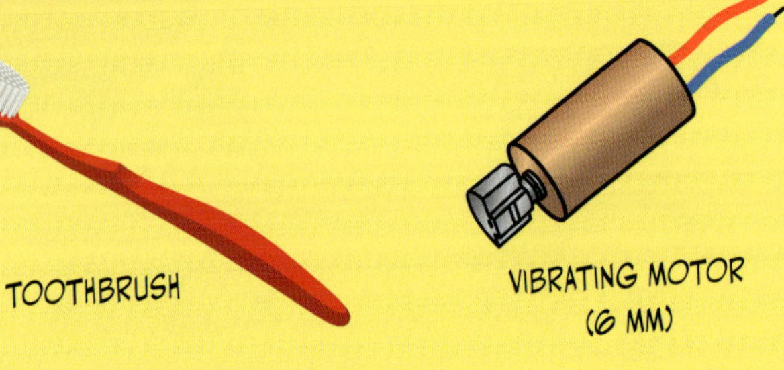

TOOTHBRUSH

VIBRATING MOTOR (6 MM)

BUTTON BATTERY (3V)

DOUBLE-SIDED TAPE

TWO PIPE CLEANERS

Ask an adult to supervise you while using a battery and electronics.

1 Ask an adult to cut the head off the toothbrush. Then stick a piece of double-sided tape along the top of the toothbrush head (the body).

2 Take the vibrating motor and stick it to the tape on top of your bot's body.

3 Take one of the wires from the motor and stick it on to the tape in front of the motor. Then stick the battery, negative side down, on top of the exposed wire sticking out of the end of the plastic.

4 Give your bug legs by bending the two pipe cleaners over its body at either end of the battery, and press them into the tape to make sure they stick firmly.

5 Test your connection. Take the other wire and touch it to the battery. Does the motor start spinning? Leave the wire touching the battery and let go – and see where your robot roves!

ROBOT OR AUTOMATON?

A little robot like this doesn't have the "brain" that bigger robots have. There's no computer program giving it instructions, so it is an automaton rather than a robot. But your bug bot does have mechanical parts (the bits of its body) and a power source (the battery), like a real robot. It won't sense its surroundings – if you let your bot bug roam freely across a table, it'll probably fall off at some point. Think about how you could adapt your mini robot, or a bigger robot made out of similar household objects, to be more "obedient."

GLOSSARY

adapt to change to meet and survive in new conditions

algorithm a set of step-by-step instructions that tells a computer what to do

allergic reaction when the body's immune system responds in an unusual way to certain plants, animals, food, etc., by making you sneeze or feel itchy, for example

anatomy the structure and parts of living things, such as all the different parts that make up the human body

android a type of robot that has a human form, which can move around

assembly line a series of machines and workers in a factory that assemble items piece by piece as an item moves along a line

astronomer a scientist who studies space and the objects in it

automaton a machine that can perform certain tasks by following a set of preprogrammed instructions

autonomous able to function and make decisions independently

component a part of something that works alongside other parts to make that thing function

cybernetics the study of control and communication in living things and in technological processes

drone an unmanned flying robot that is controlled by a human on the ground

ethical relating to whether things are morally right or wrong

feedback loop a system that links the cause and effect of an action, where some of the output is fed back into the system as input

geologist a scientist who studies the physical makeup of Earth, such as the rocks on and below its surface

humanoid describing machines that look and behave a bit like humans

inanimate describing things that aren't alive

infrared a type of radiation (energy) often given off by heated objects

mimic to copy the characteristics or behavior of something

organism any living thing

piston a short cyclinder that moves up and down inside a bigger cylinder to power a machine

radioactive describing something that has dangerous levels of radiation – an energy that can seriously harm or kill people

raw data information that has not been processed or analyzed yet

robotics the science of developing, designing, and building robots

sensor a device that detects and responds to physical things

stereo vision sight that comes from two sources, such as eyes or cameras, that combine to allow the viewer to see depth, in three dimensions

submersible describing things that work underwater

surveillance the act of watching people secretly

ultraviolet a type of radiation (energy) that cannot be seen by the human eye

weld to heat up pieces of metal so they start to melt and can be joined together

FURTHER READING

BOOKS

About Robots (So Many Questions)
Sally Spray (Wayland, 2021)

A Robot World
Clive Gifford (Franklin Watts, 2019)

Intelligent Robots (Explore AI)
Sonya Newland (Wayland, 2021)

Robots (Adventures in STEAM)
Izzi Howell (Wayland, 2017)

Working with Computers and Robotics (Kid Engineer)
Sonya Newland (Wayland, 2020)

WEBSITES

Find out more about robots on these websites:

www.bbc.co.uk/newsround/49274918
Discover more about what AI is and what it does.

www.factmonster.com/dk/encyclopedia/science-and-technology/robots
Explore more about roving robots with Fact Monster.

https://science.howstuffworks.com/robot6.htm
Find out about the relationships between robots and AI.

INDEX